OFFICIALLY
WITHDRAWN

Joshua Tree Branch Library
6465 Park Blvd
Joshua Tree, CA 92252

Table of Contents

Can you find these words?

basket

court

teammate

uniform

Let's Play!

I play basketball.

3

I wear a **uniform**.

uniform

I am on a team!

I dribble the ball.

court

It bounces on the **court**.

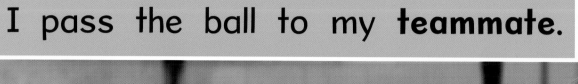

I pass the ball to my **teammate**.

teammate

She shoots the ball.

9

It goes into the **basket**.

basket

Score! Our team earns points.

Sometimes we win.
Sometimes we lose.

12

We always have fun!

Did you find these words?

It goes into the **basket**.

It bounces on the **court**.

I pass the ball to my **teammate**.

I wear a **uniform**.

Photo Glossary

 **basket** (BAS-kit): A hoop with a hanging net attached to a backboard at each end of a basketball court.

 **court** (kort): An area where sports such as basketball are played.

 **teammate** (teem-mate): Someone who is a member of your team.

 **uniform** (YOO-nuh-form): A special set of clothes worn by all the members of a team or group.

Index

About the Author

Elliot Riley is the author of dozens of books for kids. When she's not reading or writing, you can find her walking by the water in sunny Tampa, Florida.

© 2019 Rourke Educational Media

All rights reserved. No part of this book may be reproduced or utilized in any form or by any means, electronic or mechanical including photocopying, recording, or by any information storage and retrieval system without permission in writing from the publisher.

www.rourkeeducationalmedia.com

PHOTO CREDITS: Cover: taka4332; p2,10,14,15: Ignacio Ruiz Casanellas; p2,7,14,15: artisteer; p2,3,5,4,8,9,11,12,13,14,15: FatCamera.

Edited by: Keli Sipperley
Cover by: Rhea Magaro-Wallace
Interior design by: Kathy Walsh

Library of Congress PCN Data
Basketball / Elliot Riley
(Ready for Sports)
ISBN 978-1-64369-052-0 (hard cover)(alk. paper)
ISBN 978-1-64369-086-5 (soft cover)
ISBN 978-1-64369-199-2 (e-Book)
Library of Congress Control Number: 2018955866

Printed in the United States of America, North Mankato, Minnesota